# My Puppy

Written by Inez Greene  Illustrated by Larry Nolte

**ScottForesman**

*A Division of HarperCollinsPublishers*

My puppy licks my fingers.

He licks my toes.

He licks my ear.

He licks my nose.

He licks my elbow.

He licks my face.

My puppy licks me
all over the place!